DANIEL BOO
COLORING BOOK

Peter F. Copeland

DOVER PUBLICATIONS, INC.
Mineola, New York

Introduction

DANIEL BOONE, the famous frontiersman, was born to Quaker parents near Reading, Pennsylvania, in 1734, and moved to North Carolina with them when he was fifteen. He loved the outdoors and learned to survive in the natural world when he was very young.

In North Carolina he found the love of his life, Rebecca Bryan. He met her at his sister's wedding in 1753, when he was eighteen and she was just fifteen. Three years later they were married. They were to have ten children and to remain together for almost sixty years.

Even before his wedding, Boone had gone on long expeditions. In the French and Indian War he had served as a wagoner in General Edward Braddock's attack on Fort Duquesne (now Pittsburgh), Pennsylvania. He went on long hunts into Kentucky and, even though he himself had once been captured by Shawnees, tried bringing his family there in 1773. His eldest son, James, was captured and tortured to death. But two years later, Boone and his family went west again, to a settlement called Boonesboro. A quarter of a century later, when Boone and other settlers had killed off much of the big game that had fed Native Americans in Kentucky for generations, he and his family moved on to Missouri. He had always admired the Native Americans and regretted that he had had to fight them. "They have always been kinder to me than the whites," he said.

His darling Rebecca, his helpmeet for almost sixty years, died in Missouri in 1813. Boone visited her grave often. Seven years later, when he himself was on his deathbed in the Saint Charles, Missouri, home of his son Nathan, he asked to be buried next to her.

Among Boone's great admirers in later years was President Theodore Roosevelt, who wrote this about him:

> With Boone hunting and exploration were passions, and the lonely life of the wilderness, with its bold, wild freedom, the only existence for which he really cared. He was a tall, spare, sinewy man, with eyes like an eagle's, and muscles that never tired; the toil and hardship of his life made no impress on his iron frame, unhurt by intemperance of any kind, and he lived for eighty-six years, a backwoods hunter to the end of his days.

Bibliographical Note

Daniel Boone Coloring Book is a new work, first published by Dover Publications, Inc., in 2006.

International Standard Book Number

ISBN-13: 978-0-486-44738-4
ISBN-10: 0-486-44738-3

Manufactured in the United States by LSC Communications
44738308   2019
www.doverpublications.com

Daniel Boone learned early on how to survive in the out-doors. His father gave him his first rifle when he was twelve.

In 1750 the Boone family moved to western North
Carolina. They settled in the Yadkin River Valley.

In North Carolina, Daniel went on his first "long hunt." By 1751 he was already a professional hunter.

In 1755 Boone served as a wagoner in General Edward Braddock's expedition against Fort Duquesne in western Pennsylvania. A hunter he met stirred his imagination with tales of the western wilderness.

He had met Rebecca Bryan, then fifteen, at his sister's wedding in 1753. They were married three years later.

During the Cherokee War in 1759, the
family fled to Culpeper County, Virginia.

In 1761, Boone took part in a campaign against the Cherokees.

In 1765, Boone had given some extra food to the wife of
Samuel Tate, an old hunter. Boone did it as a kindness,
but Tate was jealous, and he and Boone got into a fistfight.

The following year, Daniel and Rebecca's fifth child, Levina, was born. They were to have ten children in all during their marriage.

In 1769, Boone went on his first long hunt in Kentucky. He and some other men were captured by Shawnees in December.

When Boone tried bringing his family to Kentucky in 1773, his sixteen-year-old son James and some other boys were attacked by Indians. James, Boone's eldest child, was cruelly tortured to death.

In 1775, Boone led a party cutting the Wilderness Road to
Kentucky. He founded a settlement called Boonesboro,
on the Kentucky River near present-day Lexington.

The following year, his thirteen-year-old daughter Jemima and two other girls were captured by Shawnee warriors. Boone followed them and rescued the girls two days later.

Boone was wounded in the ankle during
a Shawnee attack on Boonesboro in 1777.

While hunting bison in February 1778, he was captured by Shawnee warriors. He was adopted into the tribe, but he escaped in June.

He led a large group of immigrants to Kentucky in 1779.
They settled at Boone's Station, not far from Boonesboro.

In 1780, Boone and his younger brother, Ned, left Boonesboro to make salt at the Upper Blue Licks. He left Ned with the horses when he went after a bear he had shot, and while he was gone, Ned was killed by Shawnees.

Boone was elected to the Virginia Assembly in 1781. In Charlottesville, he and another man were captured briefly by British soldiers.

In one of the last battles of the Revolutionary War, Boone and a company of Kentucky militiamen were ambushed by Native Americans at the Upper Blue Licks in August 1782. Boone's second child, the twenty-three-year-old Israel, was killed by a bullet.

Boone and his family moved to Limestone
(now Maysville), Kentucky, on the Ohio River,
around 1783. He and his wife opened a tavern.

In 1786 he was put in command of a company
of men who attacked the Shawnee towns on the
northern side of the Ohio River.

The Shawnees and the settlers had both taken prisoners. At Limestone in 1787, Boone helped in a prisoner exchange. Many of the white women and children wept at being separated from the Native Americans they had come to love.

In 1789 Boone moved his family to Point Pleasant, in what is now West Virginia. He served again in the Virginia Assembly in 1791.

Boone was sick of trying to earn money through business deals and sick of civilization. He and Rebecca moved to a cabin and lived off the land again. Because his body was aching with rheumatism, he focused more on trapping beaver than on hunting.

He and Rebecca moved back to Kentucky and lived in a hunter's camp with two of their daughters and their husbands. Rebecca sometimes went out hunting with him, carrying his rifle when his rheumatism kept him from doing it himself.

In 1799 Boone and his family left Kentucky to settle in Missouri, which was still wild. Missouri was under Spanish rule. The Spanish were happy to have the famous frontiersman in their territory.

In 1800, the Spanish governor appointed Boone "syndic" (judge and jury) of the Femme Osage region of Missouri.

It is said that when Boone was seventy-eight years old he volunteered to serve in the War of 1812. The recruiters told him he was too old.

Boone's beloved wife, Rebecca, died in 1813.
They had been together more than fifty years.

Boone lived on till 1820. He died at his son Nathan's house, with Nathan and his daughter Jemima holding his hands. He was buried next to Rebecca in a cemetery near Jemima's farm, but his remains were later moved to Kentucky.